Yellowstone
Like no other place on earth

Featuring excerpts from Discovery of Yellowstone: The Washburn Expedition

Photography by David William Peterson

FARCOUNTRY
PRESS

EDITORIAL NOTE: This book is a photographer's tribute to the first organized survey—the Washburn-Doane Expedition—of the remarkable lands that now form Yellowstone National Park. The year was 1870 when Lt. Gustavus Doane headed a military escort of ten men who accompanied the explorers led by Montana Territory Surveyor General Henry Washburn. Nathaniel Pitt Langford, employed by financier Jay Cooke, organized the expedition to help promote Cooke's proposed Northern Pacific Railway that would pass through the area. Besides Washburn and Langford, the explorers included businessman Samuel Hauser, attorney Cornelius Hedges, writer Walter Trumbull, ex-internal revenue assessor Truman Everts, freight-company owner Warren Gillette, retailer Benjamin Stickney, and ex-millionare (from the Nevada silver rush) Jacob Smith. Their trek through Wonderland lasted from August 17 through September 21. At the very end of the journey, they came up with a totally unprecedented idea: a national park. No nation in the world had one of those in 1870.

Quotations throughout come from the journal kept by Langford, later the park's first superintendent. If they whet the appetite for the rest of the story, readers should turn to *The Discovery of Yellowstone Park*, by Nathaniel Pitt Langford, with Foreword by Aubrey L. Haines, published by University of Nebraska Press in 1972. It includes the entire journal and other writings that tell how the park came to be.

ISBN 1-56037-207-9
Photographs © David William Peterson
© 2002 Farcountry Press

Created, produced, and designed in the United States. Printed in Korea

Above: Grazing moose in the Canyon area.

Title page: Midway Geyser Basin.

Front cover: Upper Firehole River.

A new idea forms

Near National Park Mountain in the Madison Junction area.

L ast night, and also this morning in camp, the entire party had a rather unusual discussion. The proposition was made by some member that we utilize the result of our exploration by taking up quarter sections of land at the most prominent points of interest, and a general discussion followed. One member of our party suggested that if there could be secured by pre-emption a good title to two or three quarter sections of land opposite the lower fall of the Yellowstone and extending down the river along the cañon, they would eventually become a source of great profit to the owners. Another member of the party thought that it would be more desirable to take up a quarter section of land at the Upper Geyser Basin, for the reason that that locality could be more easily reached by tourists and pleasure seekers. A third suggestion was that each member of the party pre-empt a claim, and in order that no one should have an advantage over the others, the whole should be thrown into a common pool for the benefit of the entire party.

Mr. Hedges then said that he did not approve of any of these plans—that there ought to be no private ownership of any portion of that region, but that the whole of it ought to be set apart as a great National Park, and that each one of us ought to make an effort to have this accomplished. His suggestion met with an instantaneous and favorable response from all—except one—of the members of our party, and each hour since the matter was first broached, our enthusiasm has increased. It has been the main theme of our conversation to-day as we journeyed. I lay awake half of last night thinking about it;—and if my wakefulness deprived my bed-fellow (Hedges) of any sleep, he has only himself and his disturbing National Park proposition to answer for it.

Our purpose to create a park can only be accomplished by untiring work and concerted action in a warfare against the incredulity and unbelief of our National legislators when our proposal shall be presented for their approval. Nevertheless, I believe we can win the battle.

I do not know of any portion of our country where a national park can be established furnishing to visitors more wonderful attractions than here. These wonders are so different from anything we have ever seen—they are so various, so extensive—that the feeling in my mind from the moment they began to appear until we left them has been one of intense surprise and of incredulity. Every day spent in surveying them has revealed to me some new beauty, and now that I have left them, I begin to feel a skepticism which clothes them in a memory clouded by doubt. SEPTEMBER 21, 1870

Above: Bull elk and harem near Biscuit Basin, Upper Firehole River.

Facing page: Emigrant Peak outside the park, where the expedition began.

*A*ll day we have had a cool breeze and a few light showers, clearing off from time to time, revealing the mountains opposite us covered from their summits half way down with the newly fallen snow, and light clouds floating just below over the foot hills…The mountains…are rugged, grand, picturesque and immense by turns, and colored by nature with a thousand gorgeous hues. AUGUST 23, 1870

*T*he mud in these springs is in most cases a little thinner than mortar prepared for plastering, and, as it is thrown up from one to two feet, I can liken its appearance to nothing so much as Indian meal hasty pudding when the process of boiling is nearly completed, except that the puffing, bloated bubbles are greatly magnified.... SEPTEMBER 1, 1870

Above: In Upper Geyser Basin.

Facing page: Washburn Hot Springs.

This has been a terrible day for both men and horses. The standing trees are so thick that we often found it impossible to find a space wide enough for the pack animals to squeeze through, and we were frequently separated from each other in a search for a route. Hedges and Stickney, in this way, became separated from the rest of the party, and after suffering all the feelings of desolation at being lost in this wilderness, accidentally stumbled upon our camp and they freely expressed their joy at their good fortune in being restored to the party.

SEPTEMBER 8, 1870

8

Above: Foggy morning in the Grant Village area, among fire-touched forest.

Facing page: Mounts Doane and Stevenson.

*O*ne of our pack horses is at once a source of anxiety and amusement to us all.… [D]uring our journey through the forest, this pony, by his acrobatic performances and mishaps, has furnished much amusement…Progress to-day could only be accomplished by leaping our animals over the fallen trunks of trees. Our little broncho, with all the spirit necessary, lacks oftentimes the power to scale the tree trunks. As a consequence, he is frequently found resting on his midriff with his fore and hind feet suspended over the opposite sides of some huge log. "The spirit indeed is willing, but the flesh is weak." SEPTEMBER 8, 1870

Above: Near Boettler's Ranch.

Facing page: Elk calf, with Castle Geyser in the background.

Bison at Fountain Flats on the Firehole River.

Mr. Hedges and I forded the Firehole river a short distance below our camp. The current, as it dashed over the boulders, was swift, and taking off our boots and stockings, we selected for our place of crossing what seemed to be a smooth rock surface in the bottom of the stream, extending from shore to shore. When I reached the middle of the stream I paused a moment and turned around to speak to Mr. Hedges, who was about entering the stream, when I discovered from the sensation of warmth under my feet that I was standing upon an incrustation formed over a hot spring that had its vent in the bed of the stream. I exclaimed to Hedges: "Here is the river which Bridger said was hot at the bottom."

SEPTEMBER 13, 1870

The country through which we have passed for the past five days is like that facetiously described by [Jim] Bridger as being so desolate and impassable and barren of resources, that even the crows flying over it were obliged to carry along with them supplies of provisions. SEPTEMBER 11, 1870

Above: Black Dragon's Cauldron in the Mud Volcano area.

Left: Seven-Mile Hole in the Canyon area.

Facing page: Bull elk in Upper Geyser Basin.

. . . $t$here is daily crowded upon my vision so much of novelty and wonder, which should be brought to the notice of the world, and which, so far as my individual effort is concerned, will be lost to it if I do not record the incidents of each day's travel, that I am determined to make my journal as full as possible, and to purposely omit no details.

SEPTEMBER 14, 1870

Left: River otter in Yellowstone Lake.

Facing page: Pilot Peak.

*...t*he creek runs through a bed of volcanic ashes, which extends for a hundred yards on either side. Toiling on our course down this creek to the river we came suddenly upon a basin of boiling sulphur springs, exhibiting signs of activity and points of difference so wonderful as to fully absorb our curiosity. The largest of these, about twenty feet in diameter, is boiling like a cauldron, throwing water and fearful volumes of sulphurous vapor higher than our heads. Its color is a disagreeable greenish yellow. AUGUST 29, 1870

Right: Clypsydra Geyser.

Facing page: Pelican Valley and the Absaroka Range from the Sulphur Hills.

*O*ne crater emits a jet of steam with hissing noise as loud as that usually heard at the blowing off of the safety valve on a steam-boat. SEPTEMBER 4, 1870

Left: Castle Geyser.

Facing page: Lower Falls from Artist Point.

22

It was again Jake Smith's turn for guard duty last night, but this morning Jake's countenance wore a peculiar expression, which indicated that he possessed some knowledge not shared by the rest of the party. He spoke never a word, and was as serene as a Methodist minister behind four aces. My interpretation of this self-satisfied serenity is that his guard duty did not deprive him of much sleep. AUGUST 26, 1870

Jake Smith was on guard three nights ago, and he was so indifferent to the question of safety from [Indian] attack that he enjoyed a comfortable nap while doing guard duty, and I have asked our artist, Private Moore, to make for me a sketch of Smith as I found him sound asleep with his saddle for a pillow. Jake might well adopt as a motto suitable for his guidance while doing guard duty, "Requiescat in pace." Doubtless Jake thought, "Shall I not take mine ease in mine inn?" I say thought for I doubt if Jake can give a correct verbal rendering of the sentence. SEPTEMBER 9, 1870

I *went around and almost under the fall, or as far as the rocks gave a foot-hold, the rising spray thoroughly wetting and nearly blinding me. Some two hundred yards below the fall is a huge granite boulder about thirty feet in diameter. Where did it come from?*

In camp today, several names were proposed for the creek and fall, and after much discussion the name "Minaret" was selected. Later, this evening, this decision has been reconsidered, and we have decided to substitute the name "Tower" for "Minaret" and call it "Tower Fall." AUGUST 28, 1870

Above: Tower Fall.

Facing page: Great Fountain Geyser.

Shoshone Geyser Basin.

*T*here are many…springs of water slightly impregnated with sulphur, in which the water was too hot for us to bear the hand [sic] more than two or three seconds, and which overflowed the green spaces between the incrustations, completely saturating the ground, and over which in many places the grass had grown, forming a turf compact and solid enough to bear the weight of a man ordinarily; but when it once gave way the underlying deposit was so thin that it afforded no support. SEPTEMBER 12, 1870

Right: Upper Geyser Basin.

Below: Mudpot near the source of Rabbit Creek.

Above: Upper Basin, Firehole River.

Facing page: Steamboat Point on Yellowstone Lake.

Yesterday [Yellowstone Lake] lay before us calm and unruffled, save by the waves which gently broke upon the shore. To-day the winds lash it into a raging sea, covering its surface with foam, while the sparkling sand along the shore seems to form for it a jeweled setting, and the long promontories stretching out into it, with their dense covering of pines, lend a charming feature to the scene. Water never seemed so beautiful before. SEPTEMBER 4, 1870

Everything around us—air, earth, water—is impregnated with sulphur. We feel it in every drop of water we drink, and in every breath of air we inhale. Our silver watches have turned to the color of poor brass, tarnished.

SEPTEMBER 3, 1870

Left: Mineral-coated pine cones in the Mud Volcano area.

Facing page: A grizzly swims in the Yellowstone River near Mud Volcano.

Above: Rabbit Creek.

Facing page: West Thumb Geyser Basin.

These springs [West Thumb Geyser Basin] surpass in extent, variety and beauty any which we have heretofore seen. They extend for the distance of nearly a mile along the shore of [Yellowstone] lake, and back from the beach about one hundred yards. They number between ninety and one hundred springs, of all imaginable varieties. Farthest from the beach are the springs of boiling mud, in some of which the mud is very thin, in others of such a consistency that it is heaped up as it boils over, gradually spreading under its own weight until it covers quite a large surface. The mud or clay is of different colors. That in some of the springs is nearly as white as white marble; in others it is of a lavender color; in others it is of a rich pink, of different shades. September 16, 1870

Above: A coyote hunting in the Hayden Valley.

Facing page: The narrows below Tower Fall.

*M*y pack horse which I rode to-day, a buckskin colored broncho, which is docile under the pack saddle, "bucked" as I mounted him this morning; but I kept my seat in the saddle without difficulty. Walter Trumbull, however, on my return to-night, presented me with a sketch which he says is a faithful portrayal of both horse and rider in the acrobatic act. I think the sketch is an exaggeration, and that I hugged the saddle in better form than it indicates. SEPTEMBER 12, 1870

*W*e have remained in camp all day, as it is next to impossible to move. The snow is nearly two feet deep, and it is very wet and heavy, and our horses are pawing in it for forage. Our large army tent is doing us good service, and, as there is an abundance of dry wood close by our camp, we are extremely comfortable....It is cold to-night, and the water in a pail standing at our tent door was frozen at 7 o'clock in the evening. SEPTEMBER 14, 1870

Above: Norris Geyser Basin.

Right: Near Madison Junction.

Right: West Thumb,
Yellowstone Lake.

Facing page:
Fountain Flats.

During the absence of Washburn and myself Mr. Hedges has spent the day in fishing, catching forty of the fine trout with which the lake abounds. Mr. Stickney has to-day made an inventory of our larder, and we find that our luxuries, such as coffee, sugar and flour, are nearly used up, and that we have barely enough of necessary provisions—salt, pepper, etc., to last us ten days longer with economy in their use. We will remain at the lake probably three or four days longer with the hope of finding some trace of Everts, when it will be necessary to turn our faces homewards to avoid general disaster, and in the meantime we will dry a few hundred pounds of trout, and carry them with us as a precautionary measure against starvation. [Truman Everts, lost from the party, wandered alone in the wilderness for thirty-seven days, injured and starving, but survived his ordeal.] SEPTEMBER 12, 1870

Left: Black bear in Tower Fall area.

Below: Cutthroat trout at Storm Point on Yellowstone Lake.

Facing page: Crystal Falls in the Canyon Area.

*I*n addition to our saddle horses and pack horses, we have another four-footed animal in our out-fit—a large black dog of seeming little intelligence, to which we have given the name of "Booby." …The poor beast is becoming sore-footed, and his sufferings excite our sympathy, and we are trying to devise some kind of shoe or moccasin for him. AUGUST 28, 1870

*W*e broke camp at half past nine o'clock, traveling along the rocky edge of the river bank by the rapids, passing thence through a beautiful pine wood and over a long stretch of fallen timber, blackened by fire, for about four miles, when we again reached the river, which here bends in a westerly direction. SEPTEMBER 20, 1870

Right: Fire is part of the forest's life cycle.

Facing page: On the Madison River.

We were roused this morning about 2 o'clock by the shrill howl of a mountain lion, and again while we were at breakfast we heard another yell. As we stood around our campfire to-night, our ears were saluted with a shriek so terribly human, that for a moment we believed it to be a call from Mr. Everts, and we hallooed in response, and several of our party started in the direction whence the sound came, and would have instituted a search for our comrade but for an admonitory growl of a mountain lion. SEPTEMBER 11, 1870

Above: Yellowstone Lake and the Sulphur Hills.

Facing page: Washburn Range and the Hayden Valley.

*W*e were standing on the side of the [Giantess] geyser exposed to the sun, whose sparkling rays filled the ponderous column with what appeared to be the clippings of a thousand rainbows. These prismatic illusions disappeared, only to be succeeded by myriads of others which continually fluttered and sparkled through the spray during the twenty minutes the eruption lasted. SEPTEMBER 19, 1870

Left: Giantess Geyser in one of its rare eruptions.

Facing page: Grand Prismatic Spring, Midway Geyser Basin.

... I hardly know where to commence in making a clear record of what is at this moment floating past my mental vision. I cannot confine myself to a bare description of the falls of the Yellowstone alone, for these two great cataracts are but one feature in a scene composed of so many of the elements of grandeur and sublimity, that I almost despair of giving to those who on our return home will listen to a recital of our adventures, the faintest conception of it. The immense cañon or gorge of rocks through which the river descends, perhaps more than the falls, is calculated to fill the observer with feelings of mingled awe and terror. AUGUST 31, 1870

Below: Yellowstone Lake.

Facing page: Calcite Springs on the banks of the Yellowstone River below Tower Fall.

Above: Upper Geyser Basin.

Top right: Near Washburn Hot Springs.

Facing page: Firehole River.

A sulphur springs'] appearance has suggested the name, which Hedges has given, of "Hell-Broth springs;" for, as we gazed upon the infernal mixture and inhaled the pungent sickening vapors, we were impressed with the idea that this was a most perfect realization of Shakespeare's image in Macbeth. It needed but the presence of Hecate and her weird band to realize that horrible creation of poetic fancy, and I fancied the "black and midnight hags" concocting a charm around this horrible cauldron. AUGUST 29, 1870

Left: A fawn hides near Tower Fall.

Below: Cutleaf daisies.

Facing page: Mount Washburn's north slope.

General Washburn rode out to make a reconnaissance for a route to the river, and returned about 3 o'clock in the afternoon with the intelligence that from the summit of a high mountain he had seen Yellowstone lake, the proposed object of our visit…This intelligence has greatly relieved our anxiety concerning the course we are to pursue, and has quieted the dread apprehensions of some of our number, lest we become inextricably involved in the wooded labyrinth by which we are surrounded; and in violation of our agreement that we would not give the name of any member of our party to any object of interest, we have spontaneously and by unanimous vote given the mountain the name by which it will hereafter and forever be known, "Mount Washburn." AUGUST 28, 1870

West Thumb Basin,
Yellowstone Lake.

On the Yellowstone Lake shoreline at West Thumb.

I presume that many persons will question the taste evinced by our company in the selection of names for the various objects of interest we have thus far met with; but they are all so different from any of Nature's works that we have ever seen or heard of, so entirely out of range of human experience, and withal so full of exhibitions which can suggest no other fancy than that which our good grandmothers have painted on our boyish imaginations as a destined future abode, that we are likely, almost involuntarily, to pursue the system with which we have commenced, to the end of our journey. SEPTEMBER 27, 1870

*W*e believed that the great cataracts of the Yellowstone were within two days', or at most three days', travel. So when we reached Cascade creek...after a short day of journeying, it was with much astonishment as well as delight that we found ourselves in the immediate presence of the falls. Their roar, smothered by the vast depth of the cañon into which they plunge, was not heard until they were before us. AUGUST 30, 1870

Upper Falls of the Yellowstone.

... *the most remarkable of all the springs at this point [West Thumb] are six or seven of a character differing from any of the rest. The water in them is of a dark blue or ultra-marine hue, but it is wonderfully clear and transparent. Two of these springs are quite large; the remaining five are smaller, their diameters ranging from eight to fifteen feet. The water in one of these latter is thrown up to the height of two feet.*

SEPTEMBER 16, 1870

Abyss Pool, West Thumb.

*A*t change of guard Gillette's *pack horse became alarmed at somethining in the bushes bordering upon the creek on the bank of which he was tied, and, breaking loose, dashed through the camp, rousing all of us. Some wild animal—snake, fox or something of the kind—was probably the cause of the alarm. In its flight I became entangled in the lariat and was dragged head first for three or four rods, my head striking a log, which proved to be very rotten, and offered little resistance to a hard head, and did me very little damage.* AUGUST 27, 1870

Moose cow and calf near Lake Village.

Soda Butte.

Left: Mount Holmes, as viewed from Gibbon Hill.

Facing page: Lower Falls of the Yellowstone River.

The place where I obtained the best and most terrible view of the cañon was a narrow projecting point [Inspiration Point] situated two or three miles below the lower fall. Standing there or rather lying there for greater safety, I thought how utterly impossible it would be to describe to another the sensations inspired by such a presence. As I took in this scene, I realized my own littleness, my helplessness, my dread exposure to destruction, my inability to cope with or even comprehend the mighty architecture of nature. AUGUST 31, 1870

Right: Canada geese in
Upper Geyser Basin.

Facing page: Fishing Cone
at West Thumb.

Yellowstone lake…seems to me to be the most beautiful body of water in the world. In front of our camp it has a wide sandy beach like that of the ocean, which extends for miles and as far as the eye can reach, save that occasionally there is to be found a sharp projection of rocks. SEPTEMBER 3, 1870

*N*ear a boiling mud pool] is a hot (not boiling) spring of sulphur, fifteen to eighteen feet in diameter, too hot to bathe in. From these we passed over the timbered hill at the base of which these springs are situated. In the timber along the brow of the hill and near its summit, and immediately under the living trees, the hot sulphur vapor and steam issue from several fissures or craters, showing that the hottest fires are raging at some point beneath the surface crust, which in a great many places gives forth a hollow sound as we pass over it. SEPTEMBER 2, 1870

Above: Firehole Falls in its namesake canyon.

Facing page: Norris Basin, with Mount Holmes on the horizon.

Left: Clypsydra Geyser in the Lower Geyser Basin.

Facing page: Barronnette Peak.

General Washburn and Mr. Hedges are sitting near me, writing, and we have an understanding that we will compare our notes when finished. We are all overwhelmed with astonishment and wonder at what we have seen, and we feel that we have been near the very presence of the Almighty. General Washburn has just quoted from the psalm: "When I behold the work of Thy hands, what is man that Thou art mindful of him!" AUGUST 31, 1870

While surveying these wonders, our ears were constantly saluted by dull, thundering, booming sounds, resembling the reports of distant artillery. As we approached the spot whence they proceeded, the ground beneath us shook and trembled as from successive shocks of an earthquake. Ascending a small hillock, the cause of the uproar was found to be a mud volcano—the greatest marvel we have yet met with. SEPTEMBER 2, 1870

Right: Old Faithful Geyser.

Facing page: The Mud Volcano area.

Geneeral Washburn, who was a few yards behind me on an incrusted mound of lime and sulphur (which bore us in all cases), and who had just before called to me to keep off the grassy place, as there was danger beneath it, inquired of me if the deposit beneath the turf was hot. Without making examination I answered that I thought it might be warm. Shortly afterwards the turf again gave way, and my horse plunged more violently than before, throwing me over his head, and, as I fell, my right arm was thrust violently through the treacherous surface into the scalding morass, and it was with difficulty that I rescued my poor horse... SEPTEMBER 12, 1870

Near Madison Junction.

*T*he stream, in its descent to the brink of the fall, is separated into half a dozen distorted channels which have zigzagged their passage through the cement formation, working it into spires, pinnacles, towers and many other capricious objects. Many of these are of faultless symmetry, resembling the minaret of a mosque; others are so grotesque as to provoke merriment as well as wonder. AUGUST 28, 1870

Above: Grizzly bear mother with yearling twins.

Facing page: Yellowstone Canyon from the brink of Lower Falls.

*W*e were convinced that there was not on the globe another region where within the same limits Nature had crowded so much of grandeur and majesty with so much of novelty and wonder. Judge, then, of our astonishment on entering this basin, to see at no great distance before us an immense body of sparkling water, projected suddenly and with terrific force into the air to the height of over one hundred feet. We had found a real geyser. In the valley before us were a thousand hot springs of various sizes and character, and five hundred craters jetting forth vapor.....

The one I have just described General Washburn has named "Old Faithful," because of the regularity of its eruptions, the intervals between which being from sixty to sixty-five minutes, the column of water being thrown at each eruption to the height of from eighty to one hundred feet. SEPTEMBER 19, 1870

Above: Gibbon River.

Facing page: Old Faithful Geyser.

I strolled for a long distance down the [Yellowstone Lake] shore, the sand of which abounds in small crystals, which some of our party think may possess some value. Craters emitting steam through the water are frequently seen beneath the surface at a distance of from forty to fifty feet from its margin, the water in which is very hot, while that of the lake surrounding them I found to be too cool for a pleasant bath. SEPTEMBER 4, 1870

Below: West Thumb Geyser Basin and Yellowstone Lake.

Facing page: Fountain Flats, Upper Firehole River.

Above: Gibbon Meadows.

Facing page: A swim in the Hayden Valley portion of the Yellowstone River.

Jake Smith to-day asked me if I expected that the readers of my diary would believe what I had written. He said that he had kept no diary for the reason that our discoveries had been of such a novel character, that if he were to write an account of them he would not be believed by those who read his record, and he would be set down as a liar. He said that he did not mind being called a liar by those who had known him well for many years, but he would not allow strangers that privilege. This ambiguous remark indicates that Jake has more wit and philosophy than I have given him the credit of possessing. SEPTEMBER 21, 1870

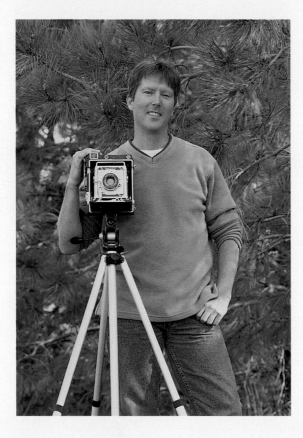

When photographing Yellowstone National Park, David Peterson often experiences a sense of déja vu. Certainly, Yellowstone's backcountry hasn't changed significantly since he first started photographing it some twenty years earlier. But maybe it's something much more mysterious—perhaps a previous incarnation? Shooting *Yellowstone: Like No Other Place on Earth* has often taken David to timeless locations throughout the park where it's hard not to imagine having explored these very same regions with the 1870 Washburn Expedition or as Nathaniel Langford, Truman Everts, or any of the other members.

Born and raised in Nebraska, David eventually moved west, where (when not working for one of the concessionaires in Yellowstone) he can be found hauling his Pentax 6x7 and Crown Graphic from one Rocky Mountain wonderland to the next. His work has appeared in *Wyoming Wildlife* and *Popular Photography,* as well as in gallery showings.